SCHOLASTIC
News
Nonfiction Readers

Venus

by
Melanie Chrismer

SCHOLASTIC INC.

New York Toronto London Auckland Sydney
Mexico City New Delhi Hong Kong Buenos Aires

These content vocabulary word builders
are for grades 1-2.

Consultants: Daniel D. Kelson, Ph.D.
Carnegie Observatories
Pasadena, CA
and
Andrew Fraknoi
Astronomy Department, Foothill College

Photo Credits:

Photographs © 2005: Corbis Images: 19 (Wolfgang Kaehler), 7 (Roy Morsch), 4 bottom left, 15 top (Galen Rowell); NASA: 5 top, 15 bottom; Peter Arnold Inc.: cover background, 5 bottom, 9 (Astrofoto), 4 top, 11 top (European Space Agency/SPL), 13 (Mark Marten/NASA), 1, 2, 11 bottom, 23 right (NASA/Science Source); PhotoDisc/Getty Images via SODA: cover, 17, 23 left.

Book Design: Simonsays Design!

ISBN 0-516-25063-9

12 11 10 9 8 7 6 5   6 7 8 9 10/0

Printed in the U.S.A.   08

First Scholastic paperback printing, October 2005

CONTENTS

WORD HUNT

Look for these words as you read. They will be in **bold**.

cloud
(kloud)

mountain
(**moun**-tuhn)

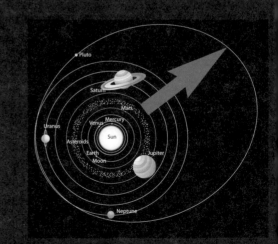

orbit
(**or**-bit)

lava
(**lah**-vuh)

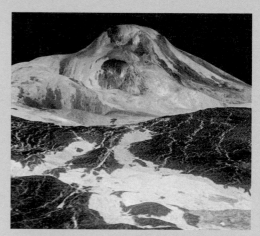

Maat Mons
(maht monz)

solar system
(**soh**-lur **siss**-tuhm)

Venus
(**vee**-nuhs)

5

Venus!

It is fun to fly a kite
on Earth.

But can you go fly a kite
on **Venus**?

No. You cannot go to
Venus at all.

Flying kites on Earth is fun.

Venus is the second planet in our **solar system**.

All of the planets in the solar system **orbit** around the Sun.

Venus is closer to the Sun than Earth. It is hotter on Venus than on Earth.

Earth

Venus

Sun

Venus is called Earth's sister. They are the same in many ways.

They are almost the same size.

They both have **clouds**.

They are both made out of rock and metal.

Earth

Venus

Venus and Earth are different, too.

The clouds on Earth are made of water.

Some of the clouds on Venus are made of acid.

The acid in some clouds on Venus would burn your skin.

Venus and Earth have **mountains** and volcanoes.

The highest mountain on Earth is Mount Everest.

The highest mountain on Venus is Maxwell Montes. It is more than 7 miles high.

The biggest volcano on Venus is **Maat Mons**.

The biggest volcano on Earth is Mount Kilimanjaro. It is 3 1/2 miles high.

Mount Everest is 5 1/2 miles high.

Maat Mons is 5 1/2 miles high.

Almost all of Venus is covered with **lava**. Lava is melted rock and metal.

Nothing lives in lava.

Almost all of Earth is covered with water.

Earth's water is filled with living things.

oceans

No, you cannot fly a kite on Venus.

But on Earth you can do many things.

You can fly a kite. You can swim in the ocean, and you can be happy you do not live on Venus!

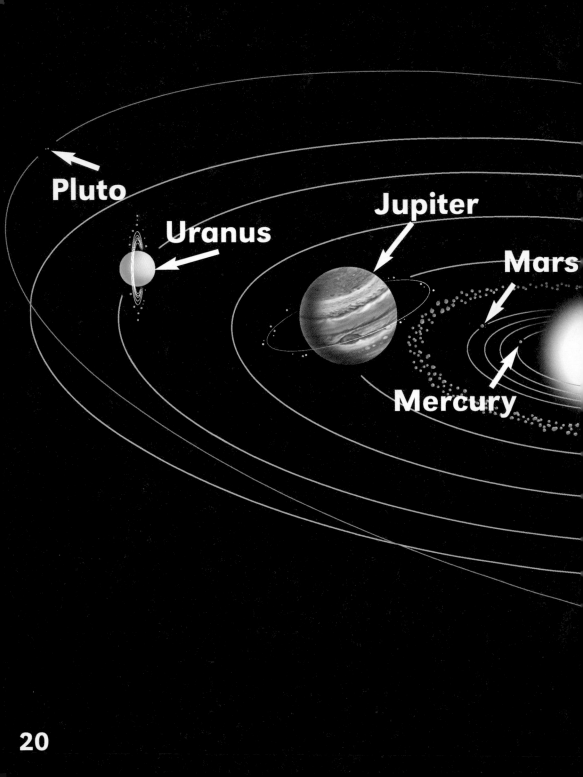

VENUS

IN OUR SOLAR SYSTEM

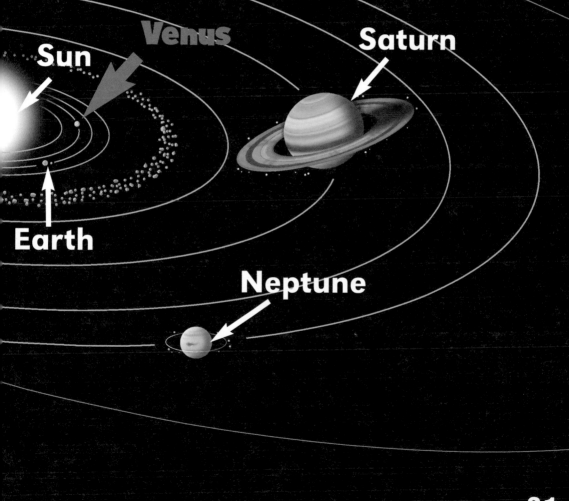

Sun

Venus

Saturn

Earth

Neptune

YOUR NEW WORDS

cloud (kloud) a mass that floats in the air

lava (**lah**-vuh) hot liquid rock that comes out of a volcano

Maat Mons (maht monz) the highest volcano on Venus

mountain (**moun**-tuhn) a high piece of land

orbit (**or**-bit) the path around an object

solar system (**soh**-lur **siss**-tuhm) the group of planets, moons, and other things that travel around the Sun

Venus (**vee**-nuhs) the planet named after the Roman goddess of beauty and love

Earth and Venus

A year is how long it takes a planet to go around the Sun.

 **Earth's year
=365 days**

 **Venus's year
=225 Earth days**

A day is how long it takes a planet to turn one time.

 **Earth's day
= 24 hours**

 **Venus's day
= 5,834 Earth hours
or 243 Earth days**

A moon is an object that circles a planet.

 **Earth has
1 moon**

 **Venus has
no moons**

Did you know astronomers have found a lava river on Venus that is over 4,000 miles long?

INDEX

FIND OUT MORE

Book:
Venus: The Second Planet
Michael D. Cole, Enslow Publishers, Inc., 2001

Website:
Venus Information and Pictures
http://www.nineplanets.org/venus.html

MEET THE AUTHOR:

Melanie Chrismer grew up near NASA in Houston, Texas. She loves math and science and has written 12 books for children. To write her books, she visited NASA where she floated in the zero-gravity trainer called the Vomit Comet. She says, "it is the best roller coaster ever!"